Original title:
Tales of the Sea's Depths

Copyright © 2025 Creative Arts Management OÜ
All rights reserved.

Author: Henry Beaumont
ISBN HARDBACK: 978-1-80587-402-7
ISBN PAPERBACK: 978-1-80587-872-8

Beneath the Glittering Surface

Bubbles rise with giggles bright,
Octopus wearing a cowboy's hat.
Fish in tuxedos dance all night,
Crabs tap their claws, how about that?

Starfish throw a disco ball,
Seahorses twirl in a wild parade.
A whale sings low, they all enthrall,
Under waves, they won't be swayed.

The Depths' Hollow Whisper

Echoes of laughter, fish a'chorus,
A clam tells jokes that are bad but true.
Jellyfish bounce on a giant surf,
Anemones giggle, 'What's new with you?'

The pirate ghost has a rubber ear,
Searching for treasure, he finds seaweed.
With every burp, the fish hold dear,
'Crabby stories' become their creed.

Ethereal Fish of Midnight

Glow-in-the-dark fish with crazy hair,
Just playing tag with a curious crab.
Waves giggle softly, a soothing air,
Mermaids toast to their night-time jab.

A ghostly ship sails through pixel beams,
With plankton dancing like it's a show.
They all burst into fits of dreams,
As the moon dips low, putting on a glow.

The Abyssal Guardian

A shark in glasses, a teacher proud,
Teaches young minnows 'how to play.'
With a flick and a swish, draws laughter loud,
While squids draw maps in a jiggly way.

Beneath the waves, humor thrives right,
Pufferfish joke about being too round.
In this realm, there's always delight,
As sea creatures frolic, joy does abound.

Waves of Lost Time

Bubbles rise, fishy pranks,
Octopus laughs, and no one thanks.
Seagulls squawk, quite absurd,
While a catfish strums a weird word.

Gill-biting jokes in the coral swirl,
Clownfish giggle, and pearls unfurl.
Lost in laughter with seaweed winks,
Sharks play tag while a mermaid thinks.

Sailor's Fables and Haunted Waters

Ghostly ships with squeaky sails,
Whispers of ghouls tell funny tales.
A pirate's parrot cracks a pun,
While a dolphin plays chase for fun.

Eerie echoes, but smiles abound,
In haunted coves where joy is found.
A crab tells tales with a wobbly leg,
As a jellyfish dances, what a beg!

The Underworld's Prism

Down where the jellybeans grow,
Colorful fish put on a show.
Mermaids play cards, laughing loud,
While sea cucumbers lead the crowd.

Shrimp compose the finest tunes,
With a chorus of picky raccoons.
In this realm of mismatched dreams,
Life is merry, nothing's as it seems.

The Depths Uncharted

In waters dark, where fish do prance,
A crab wore shoes, and took a chance.
He danced a jig with flair so bright,
While seahorses laughed at his delight.

A whale once lost his singing tune,
Complained it sounded like a raccoon.
His friends just laughed and sang along,
As dolphins chattered a silly song.

Murmurs of the Deep Blue

An octopus with eight left feet,
Joined a waltz, but missed the beat.
A dolphin giggled, made a splash,
Said, 'How about a belly smash?'

The anglerfish with glowing light,
Dreamed of being a star at night.
But all that shimmer caught a hook,
As fishy friends just had to look.

Gales and Ghosts

There were sea ghosts with sheets all white,
Trying to scare a clam one night.
But the clam just yawned, not phased at all,
Said, 'Scare someone else, my friend, not my call!'

A ship sailed through with sails so bright,
Carrying jellybeans for a snack tonight.
The crew all laughed, a comical bunch,
As they tossed sweet treats for a candy crunch.

Beneath the Tempest

Beneath the waves, where chaos churns,
A fish gave speeches, but none would learn.
His gills went flappin', words all a mess,
As waves rolled in and made him less.

A shark in shades, too cool for school,
Sipped seawater, played it cool.
With a wink and a grin, the ocean he ruled,
While tiny minnows giggled and drooled.

Shadows in the Blue

In waters where fish giggle and dance,
A crab wore a hat, taking a chance.
A dolphin played poker with a wise old shark,
Betting shiny shells till well after dark.

Octopuses juggle with shells in the tide,
While starfish spin tales of the pranks they hide.
With laughter and bubbles, the ocean's alive,
In this underwater dive, it's hard to survive!

Depths of Forgotten Dreams

A mermaid once dreamed of shoes with a heel,
But tripped on a seaweed and lost her appeal.
Jellyfish giggled, gave her a scare,
As they floated past with their squiggly flair.

The whales sing ballads, off-key and loud,
While fish form a chorus, feeling quite proud.
In the depths' silly whirl, dreams swirl and spin,
Gleaming with laughter, as joy creeps in!

Coral Keepsakes

In coral reefs, treasures are found,
A shoe from a sailor, still lost and unwound.
Clams tell of ships that sailed far away,
While sea urchins giggle at what they would say.

A lighthouse forgot where it shone in the night,
So it turned into disco, what a silly sight!
With colors and laughter, the sea's quite a show,
A party of sea creatures put on a glow!

Voices from the Deep

Diving down low, I heard fish pretend,
"Who needs a boat? We'll just swim to the end!"
A frog joined the fun with a croak out of key,
While turtles debated the best way to flee.

Squid wrote a novel, but ink got away,
As it floated around, turning night into day.
Echoes of laughter bled deep in the blue,
With voices that tickle, bringing joy anew!

Spirits of the Swell

Beneath the waves, a fish wore shoes,
It danced a jig with nothing to lose.
A crab in a hat, quite fancy indeed,
Swayed to the rhythm, with no hint of speed.

A dolphin declared, 'I can sing!'
But all that it did was make the sea cling.
The octopus laughed, inked up a tune,
While turtles blinked under a cheeky moon.

Haunting the Sand

Ghost crabs race under the moon's soft glow,
"Tag, you're it!" they shout, moving to and fro.
A seagull squawks out a spooky old tale,
While the sandcastles quiver, trembling with fail.

A hermit crab grins, in a buttoned up shell,
Says, "This sandy party's going quite well!"
With burps from the surf, and giggles unheard,
They toast to the night with a seaweed absurd.

Water's Unfathomed Stories

The fish formed a club, all wearing cool shades,
Complaining of whales and their soap opera raids.
They tossed out old nets for a grand charade,
While the eels whispered secrets they'd long since betrayed.

The starfish recounted a bumpy night trip,
When a jellyfish tried to join in the hip.
"Oh, squid, you're too shy, add some flair to this boat!"
But it swam away, wrapped in its own note.

Fables in the Foam

On the crest of a wave, a pirate once sneezed,
His parrot flew off, shocked and displeased.
With a hook for a hand and a treasure of crumbs,
He found it was tricky to navigate drums.

Crashing waves echoed with laughter and cheer,
As lobsters enacted their hilarious revere.
They tangoed to bubbles, while shells fell in line,
A comedy night, where fish orders wine!

The Mariner's Soliloquy

Oh, how I miss my pants so blue,
Lost them to a shark, it's true!
He wiggled, giggled, and swam away,
Now I fish in my undies, hey!

The gulls are laughing at my plight,
They steal my lunch in plain sight.
With breadcrumbs tossed, they dive and swoop,
While I just stand, a soggy stoop!

A crab once tried to steal my cap,
While I napped, he made a trap.
With claw and grin, he made a claim,
But I just tickled him, what a shame!

And when the waves begin to swell,
I ride them like a circus bell.
"Hold on tight!" I always shout,
As overboard, my fears cast out!

Secrets of the Sunken Realm

There's treasure lost beneath the waves,
But fish are just mischievous knaves.
They tease and wiggle, swim around,
While I'm just searching for lost ground.

An octopus stole my shiny ring,
And now he thinks he's quite the king.
I tried to barter with a shell,
He just laughed, "No, go to swell!"

A dolphin danced with glee on deck,
He flipped and flopped, oh what the heck!
I accidentally slipped and fell,
And landed right in his fishy shell!

Beneath the depths, it's filled with pranks,
Where every fish and crab just janks.
Life's a joke in the underwater zone,
I should've just stayed at home alone!

Dance of the Dark Currents

The currents twist like a wild dance,
A fish just made a foolish prance.
It twirled away, caught in its game,
While I just wobbled, feeling tame.

A seaweed monster gave a shout,
"Come dance with me," it laughed and pout.
But I just tripped, fell on my face,
And swam away with the fastest grace!

The jellyfish glow like disco lights,
While I avoid their stinging bites.
"Let's boogie down!" they start to tease,
But I swim away, quick as a breeze!

In swirling depths, the laughter grows,
As fish tell jokes nobody knows.
I float along, a clueless fool,
And join the fun without a drool!

Legends of the Ocean's Floor

They say a whale blew bubbles of gold,
As goofy tales from the deep unfold.
But I just found an old shoe instead,
With fishy dreams inside my head!

The starfish wink, they share their plots,
"Let's start a band!"—they dance and trot.
But I'm off-key, not quite a star,
My clam shell mic won't travel far!

A turtle bragged about his speed,
But tripped on coral, oh heed indeed!
He rolled and tumbled, gave a laugh,
And said, "I'm just training for my half!"

With every wave, a story's spun,
While crabs tell jokes, they're full of fun.
Deep in the ocean, smiles abound,
When silliness is the best we've found!

Beneath the Calm

Bubbles rise in a silly dance,
A fish put on a feathered pants.
The crab cracks jokes while doing a jig,
While turtles laugh with a goofy gig.

The seaweed sways in a bright green glee,
As dolphins tease the old tarpon's knee.
A starfish tries to do the twist,
But flops around, whoosh! — he can't resist.

From the Ocean's Shadow

In the dark, where shadows creep,
Octopuses snore while the fishes peep.
A whale hums a tune, quite out of tune,
While squids giggle at the buffoonish moon.

Crab conspiracies whisper and hide,
A shark in a tux, with nowhere to glide.
They play charades, though none know the rules,
How can one win when they're all just fools?

Beneath the Storm's Song

The storm arrives with a raucous cheer,
As fishes spin like they've had too much beer.
A seagull squawks words all askew,
While the clam shakes its shell like a cabaret crew.

Wave after wave, they dance and sway,
Bubble parties form in a tempest's array.
A kraken holds an umbrella, quite dapper,
And flings water with a hilarious clapper.

The Forgotten Sail

A shipwreck laughs with a rusty grin,
Sardines nestled in its rotting skin.
Anemones play tag on the worn-out mast,
While barnacles hum of the good times past.

Little fish swim in and out of the hole,
Claiming the ship as their new found goal.
With treasure maps scribbled on seaweed so bright,
They plot their adventures deep into the night.

Lighthouses and Lost Souls

In the foggy night they flash,
Seagulls squawk, oh what a clash!
A lighthouse keeper tells his jokes,
To help with all the blurry folks.

But lost souls wander all around,
Stumbling on the foggy ground.
They trip on crabs and laugh out loud,
As lighthouses glow, so brave and proud.

The ghosts complain of dull old chores,
While fishing boats pull in the oars.
With nets of laughter, they catch the fun,
In bright moonlight, they all outrun.

So next time you hear a ghostly cheer,
Just know they're laughing, never fear!
For in this world beneath the stars,
Even lost souls find their laughs in jars.

Tide Pools of Memory

In the tide pools where life peeks through,
Starfish dance, each a royal crew.
With sea cucumbers wiggling about,
One gives a wink, there's never a doubt.

Crabs in a race, oh what a sight,
They pinch each other with all their might.
A hermit crab drags a cozy shell,
Singing out loud, you know it well!

A fish with glasses earns some pay,
Sells seashells with a hip, chic sway.
While seaweed floats like hair in dreams,
The memories swirl in salty streams.

In this vibrant world, laughter grows,
With every splash, another joke throws.
In tidal pools of joy we find,
Silly wonders and waves intertwined.

The Mermaid's Grief

A mermaid once lost her shiny comb,
It sank too deep, she sighed, 'My home!'
She searched in bubbles, giggling fish,
But all they did was swish and swish.

She moped and moaned, a sorrowful tune,
Cried to the turtles, 'I'll never swoon!'
With seaweed curtains, she missed her flair,
Entered a crab with a chuckle to share.

'Oh lady fair, let's make a plan,
We'll find that comb, just bring a fan!'
Together they danced on the ocean floor,
While fish gathered 'round, calling for more.

In wacky antics, her grief turned light,
With laughter and friends, her heart took flight.
For in the depths, fun is not far,
Even lost treasures become a star.

Sheltered in Storms

When the storms come howling, drums of the sea,
Fish throw a party, wild and free.
They rattle their scales in a bubbly dance,
While sailors hold fast, gone into a trance.

A whale sings loudly, a jolly old bard,
His song travels far, he's never barred.
Then octopuses juggle with glee,
Holding up ships like cups of tea!

Amongst the chaos, a crab wears a hat,
Declares himself the captain, imagine that!
With each wave crashing, they burst into song,
Having a ball, where they all belong.

So when the storms roar and thunder aloud,
Join the fish fest, it's never too loud.
For sheltering storms can bring out the fun,
With laughter abounding, the day is won!

The Kraken's Embrace

A tentacle wraps 'round my snack,
I scream for help, but wait... what's that?
A ticklish touch from below,
This kraken's just here for my doughnut show!

With eyes that sparkle like jellybeans,
He offers seaweed for fancy cuisines.
I share a laugh, we dance with glee,
Who knew a monster liked tea with brie?

Beneath the Surface

Bubbles pop, fish start to chat,
A dolphin swims in a bright red hat.
"Why so serious?" he winks with pride,
I reply, "These sea cucumbers are my guide!"

They gossip about an ancient shark,
Who thinks he's cool but sings like a lark.
Underwater pranks, all laughter and cheer,
Who knew being submerged could bring such a career?

A Voyage into Darkness

In the depths where sunlight seems rare,
I tripped on a crab with quite the flair.
"Excuse me, mate!" he snapped with a frown,
I laughed so hard, I almost drowned!

The anglerfish offered a joke so grand,
I couldn't see it! I just needed a hand.
As we meandered through thick, murky sea,
We made light of life that's not meant to be free.

Coral Reefs and Forgotten Dreams

In coral castles where colors just pop,
A grouper wearing glasses calls me to hop.
He shows me a treasure, old shoes galore,
"Perfect for dancing," he shouts with a roar!

With seahorses twirling on invisible strings,
And starfish who moonlight as underwater kings,
We laugh at the nonsense, the dreams that we share,
In a world full of wonders, with fish everywhere!

Ghosts of the Forgotten Fleet

In a ship so old, with sails full of holes,
The crew plays cards with stubborn moles.
The captain sneezes, the ghost does swirl,
A parrot laughs, it's a spooky whirl.

They sail for pearls, but fetch some weeds,
Each treasure found is mixed with seeds.
A mermaid giggles, she's lost her comb,
In a ghostly ship, now everyone roams.

The lantern flickers, the shadows dance,
As kitschy rivals, they take their chance.
A ship of dreams, with tales that tease,
Where phantoms chuckle and do what they please.

A cheers to the crew of wobbly fate,
With jellyfish jello upon each plate.
A hearty ruckus on water's stage,
As laughter echoes through every age.

Legends of the Shallow Grave

In a cove where the fish tell their fibs,
Lurks a pirate with funny jibs.
He buried gold but lost his map,
Now he haggles with a sleeping cat.

The secrets of sand are all a blur,
While crabs recite lines, they never defer.
Shells hold stories of a clam's big dream,
While a snail insists it's faster than steam.

Old fish tales spin like a crackling yarn,
Of a mermaid who dances in a sea of barn.
With every splash, the waves start to groove,
As the seaweed sways and the dolphins move.

Beneath the waves, where bubbles rise,
Silly shenanigans just magnify.
They think they're legends, but it's quite plain,
The shallow grave's nothing but a fishy gain.

Trysts with Tides

Down by the shore, where giggles collide,
The waves have secrets they can't confide.
A clam proposes, with a pearl so bright,
While the seaweed dances in moonlight's delight.

Octopuses play games of tag with delight,
While seahorses gossip and share their plight.
The crabs all wear hats, oh what a show!
As jellyfish glow in the afterglow.

The tides whisper softly, a rhythm so sweet,
With sandcastles crumbling, a hilarious feat.
As fish put on plays in their watery spot,
The audience cheers for the jokes that they trot.

So raise a fin, to the laughter we find,
In watery places where joy is unconfined.
With each tide's embrace, and every splashy stride,
The humor of oceans excites with pride.

The Ocean's Ancient Echoes

In depths where sunlight loves to tease,
Echoes of laughter ride on the breeze.
The fish have parties in brightly strung lights,
While starfish dance to the moonlit sights.

A whale tells tales that stretch for miles,
Of underwater pranks that never get stale.
The squid holds court with ink and a grin,
While sea cucumbers wiggle and spin.

With turtles in bowties and crabs that rap,
They throw a fine bash in the coral's lap.
Where sea urchins jive and dolphins quote prose,
Each ancient echo inevitably grows.

So grab a conch shell and listen right close,
To underwater giggles, all merry and gross.
For in this deep realm of mirthful fun,
The ocean's ancient echoes have only begun.

Secrets of the Abyss

In the deep where fish wear hats,
They play cards with chatty spats.
A squid spills ink to hide his bluff,
But the octopus calls, saying, "That's rough!"

A crab in boots struts with pride,
While a fish takes a tiny ride.
Mermaids giggle, sharing glee,
As dolphins dance, wild and free.

What's that bump? A whale in disguise,
Trying on sunglasses, oh what a surprise!
The seaweed laughs as it sways with glee,
The secrets here are wilder than we.

Echoes from the Ocean Floor

Hear the clam's gossip, all the chatter,
While clowns of the reef swim, making a splatter.
A starfish sings of dreams gone by,
And jellyfish glow as they float on high.

Seahorses argue about who's the best,
One says, "Look at me, I'm simply the zest!"
A shipwrecked boot, they call their throne,
Echoes of laughter in every bone.

A riddle floats amongst the waste,
"What's a fish's favorite style of taste?"
The answer bubbles, making it clear,
Sea snacks and jokes, all through the year.

Dancers in the Dark Water

In the twilight where shadows sway,
Fishy dancers come out to play.
With twirls and spins, they steal the night,
Making waves with sheer delight.

An octopus leads in a top hat neat,
As turtles tap-dance on sea-foam feet.
A pirouette from an anglerfish bright,
Setting the mood, oh what a sight!

The deep sea ballroom hosts a large crowd,
With laughter and music, it's artfully loud.
A crab takes a bow, the limelight is craved,
In the dark water, happiness waved.

Mariner's Folklore

Once a sailor lost his way,
Chased by fish with something to say.
A barb-tailed shark wore a sailor's cap,
And said, "Mate, take a little nap!"

An old boat grumbled, giving advice,
"Watch for the wave, it won't be nice."
But seagulls squawked with raucous cheer,
"Steer for the fun, don't show any fear!"

Ghost crabs tell tales of treasure hidden,
While mermaids giggle, their laughter unbidden.
The potion of humor stirs the tide,
In mariner's tales where joy must abide.

Shadows of the Deep

In the dark where fish do flirt,
A crab in sunglasses, quite the nerd.
He tells a tale of a lost shoe,
It's very wet and quite askew.

A jellyfish with disco lights,
Dances wildly, oh what sights!
While octopuses juggle fish,
Their slippery slime—a funny dish.

A whale sings karaoke tunes,
While dolphins spin like cartoon moons.
The underwater party's quite a blast,
But don't invite the shark—he's a social cast!

So when you dive into the blue,
Remember the laughter lurking too.
For even deep below the waves,
There's giggles shared in watery caves.

Treasures Lost to Time

A chest of gold that's filled with bread,
The pirates laughed, their faces red.
'Who needs jewels? We want a feast!'
And then they danced like maniac beasts.

A compass spinning like a top,
Pointed right to a candy shop.
With lollipops and gummy bones,
They sailed the waves in ice cream cones.

Buried maps with jelly stains,
Where treasure hunters have no brains.
They dig up sandcastles instead,
Then sit and snack on crumbs of bread.

So if you think of gold and fame,
Just know they play a silly game.
For treasures lost are treasures found,
In laughter's echo, joy's profound.

The Pearl's Secret Song

Deep in a shell, the pearl does hum,
A melody that makes fish strum.
The sea turtles tap their toes,
While the clownfish strike a pose!

A swordfish dons a tiny hat,
And dances with a floppy cat.
The seaweed sways to every beat,
As stingrays shuffle their sandy feet.

The mermaids join in song and cheer,
Nodding heads from ear to ear.
While sea urchins spin with glee,
It's quite the underwater spree!

So when you're lost in ocean's throng,
Just listen close for the pearl's song.
For in its notes, we'll find delight,
In ocean's laughter, day or night.

Stories Carried by the Current

Catch a wave of laughter, ride the flow,
Fish whisper secrets, 'Did you know?
A crab once wore a pirate hat,
And danced with a hefty acrobat!'

Seahorses spin in fancy dress,
While starfish argue who's the best.
'I'm a five-point star!' one will prance,
But the others claim it's all by chance.

Currents swirl with giggles bright,
As pirates chase a watery light.
Through bubbles thick with stories bold,
They share their tales of stinky gold.

So drift along, in rippling glee,
Listen close to what you see.
For the ocean's quirk is deep and wide,
With stories that flow like the rising tide.

Fables from the Deep

There once was a fish with a curious grin,
Who claimed he could dance with a big rubber pin.
The octopus laughed, with eight arms all twirled,
And said, "You can't dance when you've got fins, my world!"

A crab wore a hat that was far too too grand,
He strutted in circles, up high on the sand.
The shells all applauded his bright, shiny show,
While nearby, a seaweed waved 'hello' below.

A dolphin named Larry who loved to regale,
Would tell fishy jokes that made everyone wail.
With puns made of bubbles and giggles that soared,
They'd roll with delight, while the sea floor adored.

The starfish on stage bought a mic from a plane,
But forgot how to use it, it drove him insane.
He sang off-key songs about his lost socks,
And laughed till the waves made him tumble in rocks.

Lagoon of Echoes

In a lagoon where the echoes play tricks,
The frogs have a band, with a frog queen who kicks.
They croak out the tunes with great hops and leaps,
While the turtles all wish they could join in the heaps.

A seagull named Pete liked to squawk with a flair,
He'd fly by the shore, giving crabs quite a scare.
"Hey, look at these shells, my feathered friends!"
They laughed with a splash as he lost in the bends.

There once was a clam with a joke book so bright,
He'd share them with everyone late into night.
He'd chuckle and shout, "Why's the sky so blue?
Because the fish keep laughing at what they can do!"

A pufferfish claimed he could float on a note,
With gills that could hum, it was quite the big boast.
But when he hit high, he inflated and squealed,
And everyone laughed as he awkwardly wheeled.

The Depths' Enchantment

A mermaid with zest wore a glittery crown,
She'd wiggle her tail in a sparkly gown.
With fishy confetti and bubbles in flow,
She'd throw the best parties for friends from below.

An octopus chef cooked with spaghetti and goo,
He'd flip flying noodles, oh what a sight too!
With sauce made of plankton and dresses of sea,
He served out delicious delights, "Come eat! Me!"

The jellyfish danced in their squishy, blue glow,
They sang about currents where silly fish go.
With umbrellas for hats, they looked quite absurd,
As they floated along, opinions unheard.

The seahorse comedian told jokes from his tank,
He'd whip out his quips, with a wink and a prank.
And all through the depths, every creature would cheer,
For laughter and fun made the ocean so dear.

Sailors' Whispers

At night when the sailors would gather for cheer,
They'd swap spooky tales, but they'd all shed a tear.
A ghost ship appeared with a crew made of cats,
Who meowed scary stories while sitting on mats.

A sailor named Tim had a fish in his boot,
He thought it was lucky, till it started to scoot.
It slipped through the deck, leaving scales in a trail,
And left all the sailors in fits of frail wail.

They'd search for gold doubloons, but oh, stuck in knots,
Their treasure was shrimps, yes, the tiniest spots!
They'd laugh and they'd cheer, "What a haul we have found!
Just wait till the cook whips up lunch all around!"

So here in the sea, where the fun never sweeps,
The sailors will joke as the ocean softly peeps.
With whispers of humor that float through the night,
They'll toast to the laughter, our spirits take flight.

Relics of the Riptide

In the water, a shoe we find,
Next to a sandwich, unbothered and blind.
A crab wears a hat, what a sight!
Dancing with fish in the pale moonlight.

A dolphin jokes, 'Don't be so blue!',
While a pirate's ghost says, 'Arrr, this is new!'
Mermaids giggle, with treasures untold,
Stealing the seaweed, their hair made of gold.

A treasure map made of drawn spaghetti,
X marks the spot, but where's the confetti?
Octopuses plan their circus show,
With jellyfish clowns putting on a glow.

And when the tide takes a playful leap,
The ocean swirls in a dance, not a peep.
Balancing fish on their fins so proud,
Under the waves, they laugh out loud.

The Whispering Tides

The waves they whisper silly rhymes,
While starfish dance to clumsy chimes.
A clam wants to sing a big opera tune,
But his shell's way too tight, oh what a swoon!

Jellyfish float like balloons in the air,
While seahorses giggle without any care.
A fish in a tux tries to catch a date,
But the mermaids just laugh, they find it so great.

The gulls tell tales with a tilt of their head,
About fish that wear hats instead of bread.
The tides keep on chuckling, rolling so wide,
Who knew the ocean had such a fun side?

As foam tickles toes on the sandy beach,
The laughter of waves is within our reach.
Every splash hides a giggle or two,
In this watery world where mirth is the view.

Ballads of the Blue

In the deep blue, fish hold a tune,
While turtles teach us the art of a swoon.
A sea cucumber struts in style,
Flipping his fins with a charming smile.

A narwhal boasts of his unicorn horn,
In tales of bravado he's quite the scorn.
The shrimps take bets on who can outswim,
Finding the ocean just wonderfully dim.

Whales croon softly, rocking the tide,
While starry skies sparkle like gems on the wide.
The crabs in a band play the coral reef,
Strumming on shells, they cause quite a brief.

And in this realm of fishy delight,
They gather at night, singing with might.
Legends of laughter, so crazy and true,
In the depths of the blue, joy never feels through.

Secrets of Silent Shores

On the shores where silence roams,
Seashells have tales that tickle like poems.
A starfish shares gossip with local clams,
While sand crabs plot their grand little jams.

The waves roll in, a sneaky parrot,
Stealing the news with a humorous carrot.
Octopus chefs whip up a feast,
With seaweed salad and oyster, at least.

A lighthouse stands, wobbly and bent,
With a light that flickers just when it's meant.
Sea turtles race, but who really cares?
They just want a nap, oh how they declare!

Every whisper of water hides laughter and cheer,
As dolphins play tag, bringing fun near.
On these shores, where time takes a break,
The secrets of life are a jolly, sweet wake.

The Depths' Delight

There once was a fish with a hat,
Who danced on a clam with a chat,
He jived with the crocs,
And pranked all the docs,
A real fishy friend, imagine that!

A crab in a tux was his pal,
Who dined on a jellyfish gal,
They feasted on cake,
But for goodness' sake,
That dessert had a very odd smell!

With bubbles that burst like balloons,
They sang silly songs to the tunes,
A walrus on drums,
Made laughable hums,
While starfish played games with the spoons!

So down where the funny fish swim,
Life's antics are never quite grim,
With gags all around,
And laughter profound,
The depth's just a joyous whim!

The Depth Beneath the Sails

A sailor with boots made of foam,
Thought seashells could be used for a home,
He built quite a mess,
Now in deep distress,
For crabs made his seashells their dome!

With mermaids who'd giggle and tease,
He'd barter for pizza and cheese,
But dolphins would flip,
And give him the slip,
In waves filled with laughter and breeze!

His parrot enjoyed shades of pink,
While squawking the oddest of things,
With jokes about fish,
That were quite delish,
They'd snicker and dance on the brink!

In waters where fun is the rule,
Unexpected shenanigans pool,
With sea shanties bright,
That spark joy and light,
This sailor's at home with the school!

Echoing Depths of Solitude

In depths so alone yet so wide,
A lonely old anglerfish cried,
His friends were all gone,
No one sang his song,
Just echoes in darkness to bide.

He conjured a party of dreams,
With mocktails and seaweed ice creams,
But lobster and ray,
Just glared him away,
As he burst out in soft, silly schemes!

With shadows that danced on the wall,
He'd throw a grand bash for them all,
But deep in the blue,
Just a couple or two,
Would snicker and shrink from the call!

Yet hope still floats up from the gloom,
With jellyfish lighting the room,
In solitude's sway,
He finds fun in play,
Crafting joy in his private costume!

Drowned Dreams

A dreamer dove deep for a wish,
He hoped to catch one on a dish,
But fish laughed and said,
"You'll go home instead,
With a pickled and speechless old swish!"

He stumbled on treasure galore,
With shiny trinkets outpour,
But crabs made a scene,
Chasing off dreams,
Now they stick to the sand on the shore!

Octopuses painting the skies,
While giggling with heart and with sighs,
They laughed at his plight,
In the murky twilight,
As he pondered more fishy goodbyes!

But still, he would dive once again,
For adventure that bubbles with fun,
In the depths, he finds peace,
As worries release,
And dances with dreams never done!

Prophecies of the Deep

A crab with glasses reads the charts,
While fish gossip, sharing smelly arts.
The octopus gives unsolicited advice,
As bubbles whisper secrets, oh so nice.

A dolphin's joke makes everyone laugh,
As seahorses dance, a silly gaff.
An old whale claims to know the stars,
But only knows them from watching bars.

Clams snicker as shadows swim past,
The seagulls wail, they're flying too fast.
A jellyfish giggles in the night,
While turtles chuckle, feeling quite light.

In these deep, silly waters we tread,
With laughter echoing, enough said!
Adventures await in the bourbon tide,
Where antics abound, and fish cannot hide.

Lost Echoes of Atlantis

Bubbles rise from a fishy feast,
As mermaids sing tunes, to say the least.
With treasure chests full of goofy gear,
They dig for laughs, not even a tear.

The city lost was filled with pranks,
Shrimp pulling jokes, with raucous swanks.
Coral reefs wear hats made of foam,
As they play bingo, far from their home.

A gnome on a raft yells, 'What's your deal?'
As sea cucumbers dance, oh what a reel!
Even the treasure maps have cracked grins,
Pointing to laughter where every joke begins.

Amidst the ruins, a giggle does dwell,
With echoes of nonsense, cast a clear spell.
In the depths, hilarity makes its home,
As garring fish frolic, no need to roam.

Sirens of the Stormy Sea

Two sirens wink from the rocks above,
As sailors pass, looking for love.
They sing silly tunes, screw up the plot,
With fish-flavored snacks that they've got hot.

A storm rolls in, the waves start to dance,
While gulls do somersaults, taking a chance.
The sailors all laugh, as masts get bent,
Making memories that're truly well-spent.

"Oooh, look at their boat!" the sirens yell loud,
As they cluck like hens, proud in the crowd.
A sailing mishap? Just a twist of fate,
While ocean characters share tricks that are great.

In the fury of waves, a gaggle takes flight,
The storm turns funny, deep into the night.
For laughter sings sweetest when seas get rough,
In this cosmic circus, we've all got enough!

Nautical Reflections

A fish in a mirror admires its scales,
While a turtle critiques, telling far-fetched tales.
"Your fins are quite fab," the clam doth jest,
As a shrimp chips in, "At least you're not dressed!"

Sunken boats boast of meetings they've had,
With dolphins and seals, who'll dance on a lad.
Old barnacles chuckle on creaky old decks,
While the laughter of seals causes no wrecks.

Reflections on water can show silly sights,
Tangled-up seaweed in playful fights.
With jigs and with japes, they spin around,
In these aquatic games, pure joy is found.

In laughter's embrace, the ocean does sway,
With giggles and snorts, it's a bright, sunny day.
For even below, where shadows do roam,
A joyful heart always finds its way home.

Tide's Silent Stories

Beneath the waves, a fish wears a hat,
Sipping seawater, now that's where it's at.
Crabs dance a jig, with shells all aglow,
While octopuses play cards, putting on quite a show.

The jellyfish jive, gliding with grace,
While sea turtles race in an endless embrace.
A mermaid's lost comb causes quite the fuss,
As seahorses giggle on a floating bus.

Anemones swear by their finest cuisine,
Puffers just giggle, "We're already so keen!"
With krill as their guests, they throw a grand feast,
But those pesky dolphins just won't let them feast!

As waves roll and tumble, the laughter will surge,
For deep underwater, the silliness will merge.
In this watery world, joy's more than a theme,
Beneath the blue surface, it's all just a dream.

The Enigma of the Deep

A clam with a secret, it's quite the detective,
Pulls shells from the ground, just feeling effective.
The fish in tuxedos, they waltz by the schools,
While the turtles just watch, thinking fish are such fools.

A conch with a sock, it's fashion's new trend,
The sea stars applaud, you can't quite offend.
But jellybeans swim with a curious grace,
Bumping into each other, all over the place.

Deep down, there's gossip, as creatures confide,
A look back at bubbles where secrets reside.
The laughter of dolphins echoes so clear,
While puffer fish giggle, "We'll swallow your fear!"

In the dark of the waters, great mysteries bloom,
With each little chuckle, it brightens the gloom.
If only the world knew how funny it feels,
To dive in their laughter among the sea reels.

Bubbles of Lost Time

With bubbles a-float, there's laughter galore,
As fish tell tall tales of what's out on the shore.
Octopuses juggle, oh what a grand sight,
While snails slug along, just trying to feel light.

A dolphin named Fred thinks he's quite the star,
He cracks silly jokes with a wink and a spar.
A tangle of seaweed he claims as his hair,
While the clownfish just giggle, not a single care.

The kraken, he snores, sleeps deep in a dream,
While the crabs pitch a fit, it's quite the grand theme.
'We need to wake him!' they plot in a line,
But all they accomplish is slipping on brine.

In this underwater, whimsical show,
Each twist and each turn makes the laughter grow.
Echoes of glee in the depths they explore,
With bubbles of joy, who could ask for more?

Ghosts of the Midnight Tide

At midnight, the pirates float by with a tease,
But their treasure's just candy — oh, they aim to please!
With hats made of seaweed and laughs made of light,
These ghosts of the tide bring such whimsy to night.

A parrot named Pete tells the best of the tales,
Of fish that take fishnets and dance with their scales.
"Can you imagine a gnome riding sharks in a race?
It'd be quite the bumpy, delightful disgrace!"

The barnacles gossip with bubbles of cheer,
While starfish spin stories that no one can hear.
Yet the shells hold their secrets, like precious old wine,
As the specters keep laughing, 'It's all been divine!'

In the moonlit embrace, the past meets the now,
For laughter's the key, and they'll show you just how.
With each splash and each swish, the echoes will play,
As the ghosts of the midnight tide dance on their way.

The Unseen Voyager

In a boat made of cheese, a sailor did dream,
He thought it might float, or so it would seem.
But the waves laughed aloud, as he paddled with zest,
While seagulls just mocked him, much to their jest.

With a map made of jelly, he sailed through the mist,
Chasing after a shark, but it just didn't exist.
He shouted, "Oh sharky, where can you be?"
His lunch floated by, like a good friend to me!

Down below, the fish giggled at the sight,
This sailor so lost, it was pure delight.
They threw him a party, with pearls and with glee,
While he swam with the dolphins, all joyful and free.

As night fell upon him, the stars sang a tune,
The moon winked and whispered, "Start home soon!"
But our cheese boat was sinking, it seemed to be sad,
Yet he laughed all the way, it was all just a fad!

Memoirs of the Brine

Once a crab with a hat claimed he owned the sea,
Inviting all fish for a grand jubilee.
They danced on the sand, on a floor made of kelp,
While octopuses juggled and whales gave a yelp.

But the crab got too proud, and he swelled up with jest,
"I'm the king of this ocean, I'm better than the rest!"
Then a wave gave a chuckle, and swept him away,
Now he tells his tale every glorious day.

An old turtle then whispered, "Let's gather the crowd,
For we all have our moments when we feel super proud."
With a wink and a splash, the fish all agreed,
That a crab in a hat was a sight indeed!

So they swam and they laughed in the moonlight so bright,
For the joys of the ocean made everything right.
With bubbles and giggles, they splished and they splashed,
In a world full of wonders, with dreams to be dashed!

Dark Waters: A Silent Saga

In the murky abyss, where the shadows loom large,
A fish with a mustache, took up a grand charge.
He proclaimed to the darkness, "I'm the one you shall see,

I'll conquer these depths, just you wait and see!"

But the octopus snickered, "Oh do take a seat,
You think you're the bravest? Oh isn't that sweet!"
With tentacles twirling, they gave him a show,
While the fish turned quite red, but still put on a glow.

A lanternfish giggled, "There's nothing to fear,
You're a star in the dark, so bring us your cheer!"
Together they frolicked, with bubbles and flair,
For in the dark waters, there's laughter to share.

And so they all danced, in the depths far below,
With the fish in his mustache, putting on quite a show.
Embracing the shadows, they twirled with delight,
For a saga of silence can also be light!

Beneath the Stormy Surface

Down below the wild waves, where the currents do swirl,
A clam dreamed of glory, and gave it a whirl.
In a shell made for champions, he planned his grand race,

Shouting, "I'll win this! Just give me some space!"

But the barnacle chuckled, "You think you can zoom?
It takes more than a dream to escape this dark gloom."
Yet the clam wouldn't listen, he took off with a splash,
While the starfish just laughed, "What a mad little dash!"

The jellyfish giggled, as they floated on by,
While the clam sailed past, like a twinkle in the sky.
With currents all swirling, and bubbles in sight,
He fell for the mischief, but oh what a fright!

For the storm came a'rolling, like a wave of surprise,
And the clam found himself in a comedy of lies.
Yet the friends all swirled closer, in this watery dance,
For beneath all that chaos, they'd each had their chance!

The Forgotten Nautilus

A nautilus lost his way,
In a shell that spun all day.
He danced with fish in a merry jig,
Claiming he was a giant pig.

His friends all giggled, oh what a sight,
As he twirled in the moon's soft light.
But one sly crab, with a crafty grin,
Whispered, "Nautilus, where have you been?"

With a wink, he promised he'd return,
To show them how the sea could churn.
But all he did was bump and roll,
This nautilus lacks ocean control.

So next time you see him swim with glee,
Remember, he's just too wobbly!
And if you hear him whoop and cheer,
It's just the seaweed tickling his ear.

The Depths of Reverie

In the deep, where dreams collide,
A fish wore glasses with great pride.
He read the currents like a book,
While seaweed shook with a curious look.

A shark swam by, quite bemused,
"What's with the specs? Are you confused?"
The fish replied, with a knowing stare,
"I'm reading up on ocean flair!"

A jellyfish floated, quite aghast,
"Wearing glasses? That won't last!"
But the fish just smiled, flipping a page,
"Knowledge, my friend, is all the rage."

And so they laughed in bubbles and trails,
While the crab sold popcorn and tickled the scales.
In these depths where giggles blend,
You'll find wisdom is a wiggly friend.

Chronicles of the Coral

In coral realms, where colors gleam,
A lobster lost his daily dream.
He searched for a sock, of vibrant hue,
Thinking it made him look brand new.

"You don't need socks!" the clownfish laughed,
"Your claws are fine, it's quite a craft!"
But Mr. Lobster with his fancy flair,
Just liked the way the fabric would wear.

A sea turtle rolled his eyes so wide,
"Fashion in the ocean? What a ride!"
Yet, under moonlight, he joined in the fuss,
Dancing with socks, amid all the muss.

So to this day, in the coral's twist,
The lobster struts, none can resist.
With vibrant socks and stylish stride,
He reigns as king in the ocean wide.

The Abyssal Songs

In the abyss, where shadows play,
A squid sang songs in a wobbly way.
His voice like bubbles, popping bright,
Made the anglerfish beam with delight.

The octopus shrugged, with arms a-twist,
"Is this a concert? Or just a tryst?"
But the squid had a plan, to take the stage,
With an audience of creatures, in this dark cage.

"Let's groove, my friends, in these murky streams!
Dance with the currents, fulfill your dreams!"
So they bobbed and swayed, in silly delight,
Creating a scene, a whimsical sight.

And now down deep, where the blackness yawns,
They have parties with deep-sea brawns.
Where laughter echoes in bubbles' air,
Who knew the abyss could be so rare?

The Call of the Deep

A clam with a shell that plays jazz,
Dances with fish that wear bright sunglasses.
The octopus has a drum and a beat,
As seahorses salsa on the ocean's street.

In coral clubs, there's a crab DJ,
Mixing tunes while the jellyfish sway.
Lobsters line up for a late-night bite,
Laughing and clapping under the moonlight.

But watch out for the grouchy old eel,
Who grumbles 'No fun!' with a slippery squeal.
He tries to be cool, but he's just a bore,
Shaking his tail, he looks like a chore.

So if you dive deep, bring your best gear,
And join in the laughter, there's nothing to fear.
The calls of the deep are nuts, I confess,
Where every fish party ends with a splash, not a mess!

Secrets of Sunken Ships

Beneath the waves, treasures are found,
With tales of pirates that jump all around.
But the mermaids giggle at their old gold,
Claiming it's cursed and far too bold.

A ship once sailed with a crew full of jest,
Who thought it would be a relaxing quest.
But they tripped on the rigging, fell on their face,
Now sharks swim by to see the strange grace.

One pirate's parrot took control of the wheel,
Squawking directions with blundering zeal.
They sailed in circles, forgot how to steer,
Now they're the ocean's laughingstock, oh dear!

Under the hull where the barnacles thrive,
The stories of giggles just seem to come alive.
Lost in the depths, they still plot and scheme,
For a treasure of punchlines, part of their dream!

The Ocean's Heartbeat

The bubbles that rise are like a tick-tock,
A heartbeat of waves dressed in seaweed sock.
Fish gather 'round for the weekly show,
Where sea turtles waddle with a flashy glow.

The dolphins perform with a splash and a flip,
Balancing beach balls on top of their lip.
The starfish cheer, giving applause with their arms,
While the crabs book tickets to watch all the charms.

But beware the deep blubbering whale's song,
It echoes for miles and goes on too long.
He sings of his childhood and weathered old shoes,
While squids keep on changing their colorful hues.

In the currents where laughter twists and twirls,
Are whispers of joy from the ocean's swirls.
Where every fin tickles and mermaids decree,
That laughter is gold in the vast, salty sea.

Nautical Nightmares

A fish with a mustache gave a loud yawn,
Dreaming of beaches with candy and dawn.
But the jelly seen dancing slipped on a fin,
And created a ruckus, oh where to begin!

The gulls squawk loudly, holding the trend,
Of stealing the snacks that the fishermen send.
With flippers and flaps, it's a chaotic scene,
As the trollers get slimed by the sea's silly queen.

Octopuses dressed like a band from the past,
Play soundtracks to battles of fish caught at last.
But the sea cucumbers just crawl and gun,
While they laugh at the shenanigans, just for the fun.

So if you see fish in silly attire,
Join in their laughter, let fun never tire.
In nightmares of waves, there's nothing to dread,
Just more wacky antics from the deep's funny thread!

www.ingramcontent.com/pod-product-compliance
Lightning Source LLC
Chambersburg PA
CBHW060144230426
43661CB00003B/566